HAL LEONARD GUITAR METHOD
Supplement to Any Guitar Method

EVEN MORE EASY POP MELODIES

INTRODUCTION

Welcome to *Even More Easy Pop Melodies*, a collection of 20 pop and rock favorites arranged for easy guitar. If you're a beginning guitarist, you've come to the right place; these well-known songs will have you playing, reading, and enjoying music in no time!

This collection can be used on its own or as a supplement to the *Hal Leonard Guitar Method* or any other beginning guitar method. The songs are arranged in order of difficulty. Each melody is presented in an easy-to-read format – including lyrics to help you follow along and chords for optional accompaniment (by your teacher, if you have one).

USING THE AUDIO TRACKS

Even More Easy Pop Melodies* is available as a book/audio package so you can practice strumming along with a real band. On the audio tracks, each song begins with a full (or partial) measure of clicks, which sets the tempo and prepares you for playing along. To tune your guitar to the audio, use the tuning notes track.

To access audio visit:
www.halleonard.com/mylibrary

Enter Code
2405-9041-7471-2212

ISBN 978-1-4950-9119-3

7777 W. BLUEMOUND RD. P.O. BOX 13819 MILWAUKEE, WI 53213

Visit Hal Leonard Online at
www.halleonard.com

SONG STRUCTURE

The songs in this book have different sections, which may or may not include the following:

Intro
This is usually a short instrumental section that "introduces" the song at the beginning.

Verse
This is one of the main sections of a song and conveys most of the storyline. A song usually has several verses, all with the same music but each with different lyrics.

Chorus
This is often the most memorable section of a song. Unlike the verse, the chorus usually has the same lyrics every time it repeats.

Bridge
This section is a break from the rest of the song, often having a very different chord progression and feel.

Solo
This is an instrumental section, often played over the verse or chorus structure.

Outro
Similar to an intro, this section brings the song to an end.

ENDINGS & REPEATS

Many of the songs have some new symbols that you must understand before playing. Each of these represents a different type of ending.

1st and 2nd Endings
These are indicated by brackets and numbers. The first time through ɑ play the first ending and then repeat. The second time through, skip tl and play through the second ending.

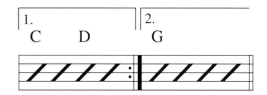

D.S.
This means "Dal Segno" or "from the sign." When you see this abbreviation above the staff, find the sign (𝄋) earlier in the song and resume playing from that point.

al Coda
This means "to the Coda," a concluding section in the song. If you see the words "D.S. al Coda," return to the sign (𝄋) earlier in the song and play until you see the words "To Coda," then skip to the Coda at the end of the song, indicated by the symbol: ⊕.

al Fine
This means "to the end." If you see the words "D.S. al Fine," return to the sign (𝄋) earlier in the song and play until you see the word "Fine."

D.C.
This means "Da Capo" or "from the head." When you see this abbreviation above the staff, return to the beginning (or "head") of the song and resume playing.

CONTENTS

ELEANOR RIGBY

Words and Music by
John Lennon and Paul McCartney

Intro

C

Ah, _____ look at all _____ the lone - ly peo -

Em — **C**

- ple! _____ Ah, _____ look at all _____

Em

_____ the lone - ly peo - ple! _____

Verse

Em

1. El - ea - nor Rig - by, picks up the rice _____ in the church _____
2. Fa - ther Mc - Ken - zie, writ - ing the words _____ of a ser -
3. El - ea - nor Rig - by, died in the church _____ and was bur -

C

_____ where a wed - ding has been, _____ lives in a dream. _____
- mon that no _____ one will hear, _____ no one comes near. _____
- ied a - long _____ with her name, _____ no - bod - y came. _____

CAN'T BUY ME LOVE

Words and Music by
John Lennon and Paul McCartney

HOME

Words and Music by
Greg Holden and Drew Pearson

home.   Verse

2. Set-tle down, _____ it -'ll all be

clear.   Don't pay no mind to the de-mons; they fill you with

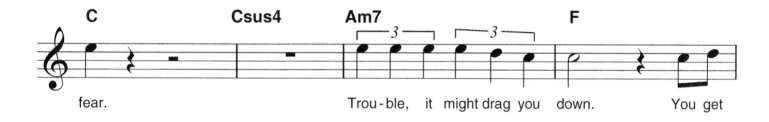

fear.   Trou-ble, it might drag you down.   You get

lost, you can al-ways be found.   Just know you're not a - lone, ___

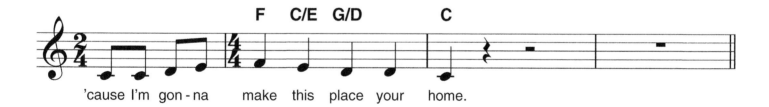

'cause I'm gon-na make this place your home.

Outro   *Repeat and fade*

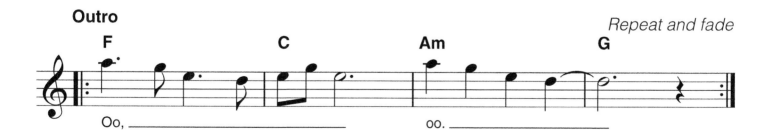

Oo, _____   oo. _____

ANOTHER BRICK IN THE WALL

Words and Music by
Roger Waters

Verse

Dm

1., 2. We don't need _ no ed - u - ca - tion.

We don't need _ no thought con - trol, _

no dark sar - cas - m

in the class - room.

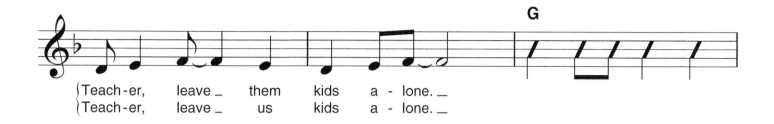

Teach-er, leave _ them kids a - lone. _
Teach-er, leave _ us kids a - lone. _

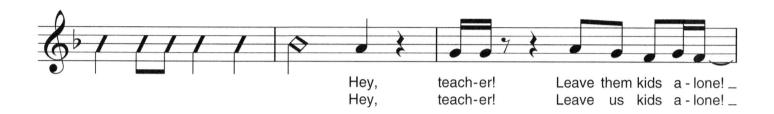

Hey, teach-er! Leave them kids a-lone! _
Hey, teach-er! Leave us kids a-lone! _

Dm ⌐3⌐ **Am G** **Chorus** **F**

——
——
All in all, __ it's just an-
All in all, __ you're just an-

C **Dm**

- oth-er brick in the wall.⌏
- oth-er brick in the wall.⌏

F **C**

All in all, ___ you're just an - oth-er brick in the

Dm

wall.

HEY, SOUL SISTER

Words and Music by Pat Monahan,
Espen Lind and Amund Bjorklund

STAY WITH ME

Words and Music by Sam Smith,
James Napier, William Edward Phillips,
Tom Petty and Jeff Lynne

Verse

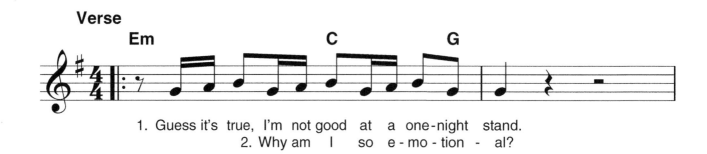

1. Guess it's true, I'm not good at a one-night stand.
2. Why am I so e-mo-tion-al?

But I still need love 'cause I'm just a man.
No, it's not a good look. Gain some self-con-trol.

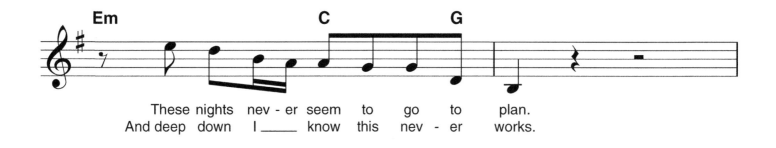

These nights nev-er seem to go to plan.
And deep down I ____ know this nev-er works.

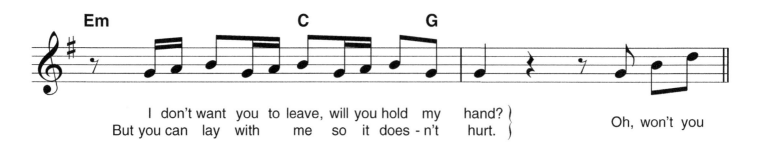

I don't want you to leave, will you hold my hand? }
But you can lay with me so it does-n't hurt. }

Oh, won't you

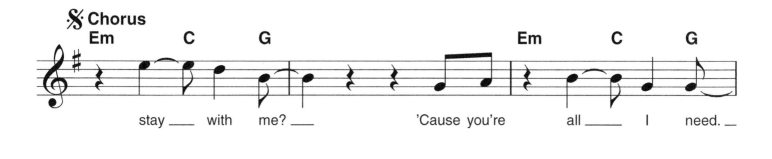

(SITTIN' ON) THE DOCK OF THE BAY

Words and Music by
Steve Cropper and Otis Redding

ANOTHER ONE BITES THE DUST

Words and Music by
John Deacon

18

An - oth - er one bites the dust. ____ And an -

oth - er one gone, and an - oth - er one gone, an - oth - er one bites the dust. ____

Hey! ____ I'm gon - na get you, too, an - oth - er one bites the dust. ____

Outro

Repeat and fade

CRAZY TRAIN

Words and Music by
Ozzy Osbourne, Randy Rhoads
and Bob Daisley

Intro

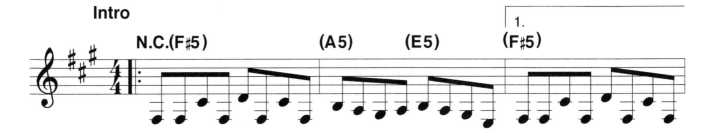

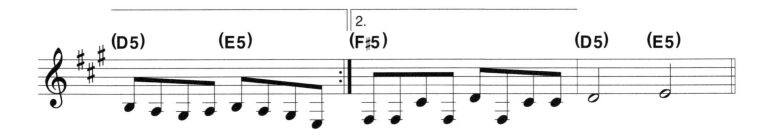

Verse

1. Cra - zy,   but that's how it goes. _____

(2.) lis - tened to preach - ers,   I've lis - tened to fools. _____   I've

Mil-lions of peo - ple   liv - ing as foes. _____

watched all the drop - outs   who make their own rules. _____

20

21

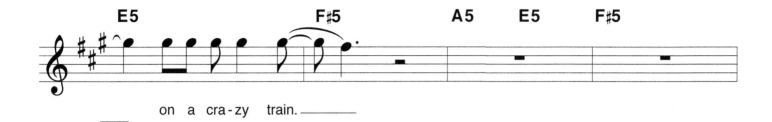

on a cra - zy train.

2. I've

Bridge

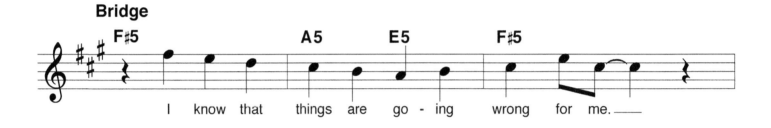

I know that things are go - ing wrong for me.

You've got - ta lis - ten to my

Guitar Solo

words, yeah, yeah!

Fade out

HEART SHAPED BOX

Words and Music by
Kurt Cobain

Drop D tuning:
(low to high) D-A-D-G-B-E

1. She ___ eyes me like ___ a pis - ces when ___
2. Meat - eat - ing or - chids for - give no ___

___ I ___ am weak. ___ I've been locked in - side ___
___ one ___ just yet. ___ Cut my - self on an -

___ your heart - shaped box ___ for ___ weeks. ___
- gels hair ___ and ba - by's ___ breath. ___

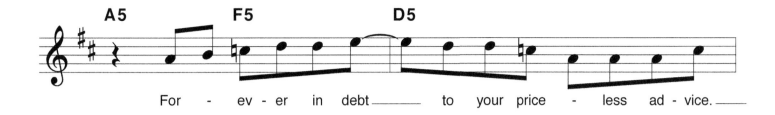

For - ev - er in debt _____ to your price - less ad - vice. _____

_____ Hey! Wait! I've got a new com - plaint.

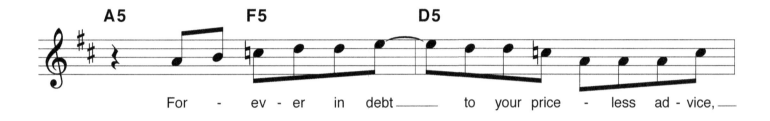

For - ev - er in debt _____ to your price - less ad - vice, _____

_____ your ad - vice. _____

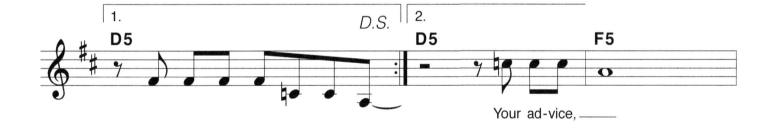

Your ad-vice, _____

your ad-vice. _____ *rit.*

RUNAWAY

Words and Music by
Max Crook and Del Shannon

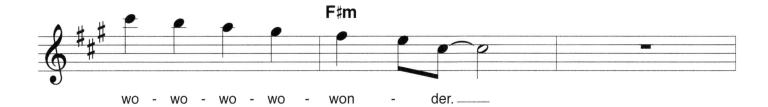

wo - wo - wo - wo - won - der. ___

Why, ___ why, why, why, why, why, she ran a - way, ___

___ and ___ I won - der where she will stay, ___

___ my lit - tle run - a - way, ___ a

To Coda ⊕   *D.S. al Coda*
                   (take repeat)

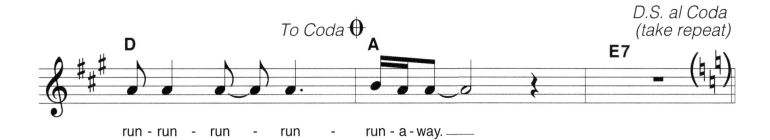

run - run - run - run - run - a - way. ___

⊕ **Coda**

Repeat and fade

run - a - way, ___ a run - run - run - run -

TEQUILA

By Chuck Rio

Intro

(spoken:) Tequila!

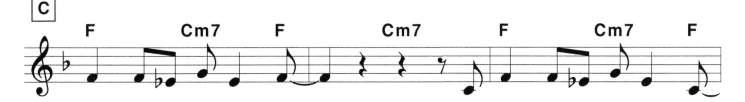

(spoken:) Tequila!

Yesterday

Words and Music by
John Lennon and Paul McCartney

GOOD VIBRATIONS

Words and Music by
Brian Wilson and Mike Love

21 GUNS

Words and Music by David Bowie,
John Phillips, Billie Joe and Green Day

Verse

1. Do you know __ what's worth fight - ing for __
2. Does the pain __ weigh __ out __ the pride __
3. *See additional lyrics*

when it's not __ worth dy - ing for? __ Does it take your
and you look __ for a place __ to hide? __ Did some-one break your

breath __ a - way __ and you feel __ your-self suf - fo - cat - ing?
heart __ in - side? __ You're in

ru - ins. __

Chorus

One, twen-ty one guns. __ Lay down your arms, __

Additional Lyrics

3. When it's time to live and let die
And you can't get another try,
Something inside this heart has died.
You're in ruins.

ROLLING IN THE DEEP

Words and Music by
Adele Adkins and Paul Epworth

think-ing that we al-most had it all. The scars of your ___ love, they leave me

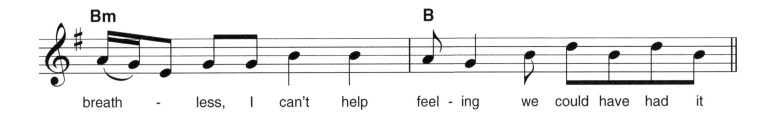

breath - less, I can't help feel - ing we could have had it

Chorus

all, _____ roll - ing in the deep. _____

___ You had my heart in - side _____ of your hand, _____ {and/but} you played ___

___ it ___ to the beat. _____ We could have had it

_____ it, you played _ it, you played _ it, you played _ it to the beat. _

HALLELUJAH

Words and Music by
Leonard Cohen

Verse

C   Am

1. I've heard there was a se-cret chord ___ that
faith was strong but you need-ed proof. ___ You

C   Am   F

Da-vid played, _ and it pleased the Lord. But you don't ___ real-ly
saw ___ her ___ bath-ing on the roof. Her beau-ty ___ and the

G   C   G

care for mu-sic, do ya? ___ It
moon-light o-ver-threw you. ___ She

C   F   G   Am

goes like this: the fourth, the fifth, the mi-nor fall, ___ the
tied you to a kitch-en chair. She broke your throne; _ she

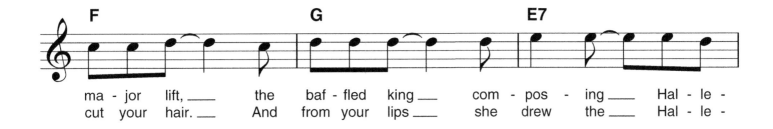

ma - jor lift,____ the baf - fled king ____ com - pos - ing ____ Hal - le -
cut your hair. ____ And from your lips ____ she drew the ____ Hal - le -

%Chorus

lu - jah. ____ } Hal - le - lu - jah, ____ Ha - le -

lu - jah, ____ Hal - le - lu - jah, ____ Hal - le -

3rd time, to Coda ⊕

lu - jah. 2. Your

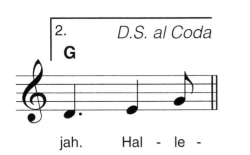

D.S. al Coda

jah. Hal - le -

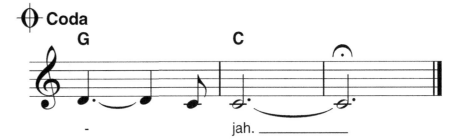

⊕ **Coda**

- jah. ____

SLEEPWALK

By Santo Farina,
John Farina and Ann Farina

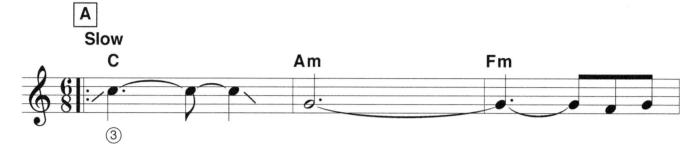

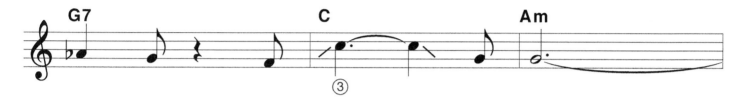

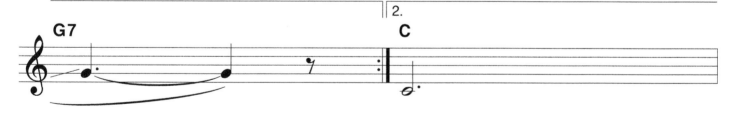

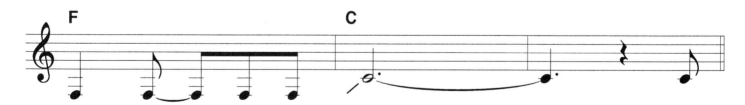

B F

Fm

C

C7

F

Fm

G7

D.C. al Coda

G7#9

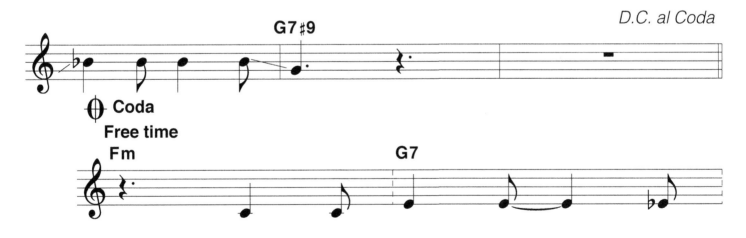

Coda
Free time
Fm

G7

G7#9   N.C.

C$_9^6$ G7$_{\sharp 5}^{\flat 9}$ C$_9^6$

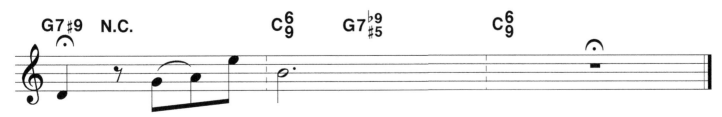

SEA OF LOVE

Words and Music by
George Khoury and Philip Baptiste

Coda

G ... N.C.

love you. ————

Chorus

Come ———— with me ——— to the sea ——

— of love. ————

Verse

4. Come with me, ——— my ——— love, — to the sea, ——— the

sea ——— of love. —— I ——— want to tell you just ——— how much I

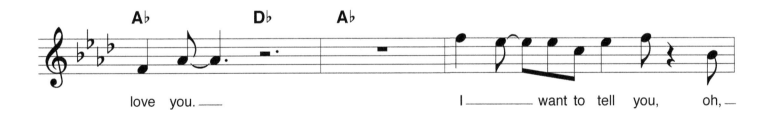

love you. ——— I ———— want to tell you, oh, —

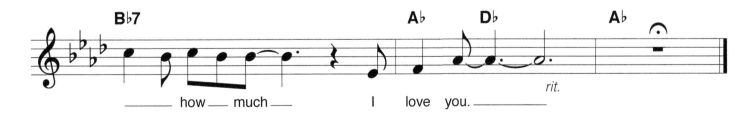

——— how — much —— I love you. ————

rit.

43

CRAZY

Words and Music by
Willie Nelson

won - d'rin' _____ what in the world did I do? _____

Chorus

_____ Cra - zy _____ for think - ing that my love could

hold you; _____ I'm cra - zy for try - in', _____

cra - zy for cry - in', _____ and I'm cra - zy for lov - in'

Chorus

you. Cra - zy _____ for think - ing that my love could

hold you; _____ I'm cra - zy for try - in', _____

cra - zy for cry - in', _____ and I'm cra - zy for lov - in' you.

HAL LEONARD GUITAR METHOD

METHOD BOOKS, SONGBOOKS AND REFERENCE BOOKS

THE HAL LEONARD GUITAR METHOD is designed for anyone just learning to play acoustic or electric guitar. It is based on years of teaching guitar students of all ages, and it also reflects some of the best guitar teaching ideas from around the world. This comprehensive method includes: A learning sequence carefully paced with clear instructions; popular songs which increase the incentive to learn to play; versatility – can be used as self-instruction or with a teacher; audio accompaniments so that students have fun and sound great while practicing.

BOOK 1
00699010 Book Only $8.99
00699027 Book/Online Audio $12.99
00697341 Book/Online Audio + DVD $24.99
00697318 DVD Only $19.99
00155480 Deluxe Beginner Edition
(Book, CD, DVD, Online Audio/
Video & Chord Poster) $19.99

COMPLETE (BOOKS 1, 2 & 3)
00699040 Book Only $16.99
00697342 Book/Online Audio $24.99

BOOK 2
00699020 Book Only $8.99
00697313 Book/Online Audio $12.99

BOOK 3
00699030 Book Only $8.99
00697316 Book/Online Audio $12.99

Prices, contents and availability subject to change without notice.

STYLISTIC METHODS

ACOUSTIC GUITAR
00697347 Method Book/Online Audio $17.99
00237969 Songbook/Online Audio $16.99

BLUEGRASS GUITAR
00697405 Method Book/Online Audio $16.99

BLUES GUITAR
00697326 Method Book/Online Audio (9" x 12") .$16.99
00697344 Method Book/Online Audio (6" x 9")...$15.99
00697385 Songbook/Online Audio (9" x 12") $14.99
00248636 Kids Method Book/Online Audio $12.99

BRAZILIAN GUITAR
00697415 Method Book/Online Audio $17.99

CHRISTIAN GUITAR
00695947 Method Book/Online Audio $16.99
00697408 Songbook/CD Pack $14.99

CLASSICAL GUITAR
00697376 Method Book/Online Audio $15.99

COUNTRY GUITAR
00697337 Method Book/Online Audio $22.99
00697400 Songbook/Online Audio $19.99

FINGERSTYLE GUITAR
00697378 Method Book/Online Audio $21.99
00697432 Songbook/Online Audio $16.99

FLAMENCO GUITAR
00697363 Method Book/Online Audio $15.99

FOLK GUITAR
00697414 Method Book/Online Audio $16.99

JAZZ GUITAR
00695359 Book/Online Audio $22.99
00697386 Songbook/Online Audio $15.99

JAZZ-ROCK FUSION
00697387 Book/Online Audio $24.99

R&B GUITAR
00697356 Book/Online Audio $19.99
00697433 Songbook/CD Pack $14.99

ROCK GUITAR
00697319 Book/Online Audio $16.99
00697383 Songbook/Online Audio $16.99

ROCKABILLY GUITAR
00697407 Book/Online Audio $16.99

OTHER METHOD BOOKS

BARITONE GUITAR METHOD
00242055 Book/Online Audio $12.99

GUITAR FOR KIDS
00865003 Method Book 1/Online Audio $12.99
00697402 Songbook/Online Audio $9.99
00128437 Method Book 2/Online Audio $12.99

MUSIC THEORY FOR GUITARISTS
00695790 Book/Online Audio $19.99

TENOR GUITAR METHOD
00148330 Book/Online Audio $12.99

12-STRING GUITAR METHOD
00249528 Book/Online Audio $19.99

METHOD SUPPLEMENTS

ARPEGGIO FINDER
00697352 6" x 9" Edition $6.99
00697351 9" x 12" Edition $9.99

BARRE CHORDS
00697406 Book/Online Audio $14.99

CHORD, SCALE & ARPEGGIO FINDER
00697410 Book Only $19.99

GUITAR TECHNIQUES
00697389 Book/Online Audio $16.99

INCREDIBLE CHORD FINDER
00697200 6" x 9" Edition $7.99
00697208 9" x 12" Edition $7.99

INCREDIBLE SCALE FINDER
00695568 6" x 9" Edition $9.99
00695490 9" x 12" Edition $9.99

LEAD LICKS
00697345 Book/Online Audio $10.99

RHYTHM RIFFS
00697346 Book/Online Audio $14.99

SONGBOOKS

CLASSICAL GUITAR PIECES
00697388 Book/Online Audio $9.99

EASY POP MELODIES
00697281 Book Only $7.99
00697440 Book/Online Audio $14.99

(MORE) EASY POP MELODIES
00697280 Book Only $6.99
00697269 Book/Online Audio $14.99

(EVEN MORE) EASY POP MELODIES
00699154 Book Only $6.99
00697439 Book/Online Audio $14.99

EASY POP RHYTHMS
00697336 Book Only $7.99
00697441 Book/Online Audio $14.99

(MORE) EASY POP RHYTHMS
00697338 Book Only $7.99
00697322 Book/Online Audio $14.99

(EVEN MORE) EASY POP RHYTHMS
00697340 Book Only $7.99
00697323 Book/Online Audio $14.99

EASY POP CHRISTMAS MELODIES
00697417 Book Only $9.99
00697416 Book/Online Audio $14.99

EASY POP CHRISTMAS RHYTHMS
00278177 Book Only $6.99
00278175 Book/Online Audio $14.99

EASY SOLO GUITAR PIECES
00110407 Book Only $9.99

REFERENCE

GUITAR PRACTICE PLANNER
00697401 Book Only $5.99

GUITAR SETUP & MAINTENANCE
00697427 6" x 9" Edition $14.99
00697421 9" x 12" Edition $12.99

For more info, songlists, or to purchase these and more books from your favorite music retailer, go to

halleonard.com

HAL•LEONARD®